TOP 10
BASKETBALL
POWER
FORWARDS

Jeff Savage

Enslow Publishers, Inc.

44 Fadem Road	PO Box 38
Box 699	Aldershot
Springfield, NJ 07081	Hants GU12 6BP
USA	UK

Library of Congress Cataloging-in-Publication Data

Savage, Jeff.
    Top 10 basketball power forwards/ Jeff Savage
        p. cm.—(Sports top 10)
    Includes bibliographical references and index.
    ISBN 0-89490-808-1
        1. Forwards (Basketball)—United States—Biography—Juvenile literature.
    2. Forwards (Basketball)—Rating of—Juvenile literature. [1. Basketball players.]
    I. Title. II. Series.
    GV884.A1S29 1997
    796.323'092'2—dc20
    [B]   96-9131
                                  CIP
                                  AC

Printed in the United States of America

10 9 8 7 6 5 4 3 2 1

Photo Credits: AP/Wide World Photos, pp. 11, 37, 41; Bill Baptist/NBA Photos, pp. 7,
26; Andrew D. Bernstein/NBA Photos, p. 31; Nathaniel S. Butler/ NBA Photos, pp. 13,
22, 25, 33; Lou Capozzola/NBA Photos, p. 45; Sam Forencich/NBA Photos, pp. 29, 42;
Andy Hayt/NBA Photos, p. 9; Naismith Memorial Basketball Hall of Fame, pp. 14, 17,
19, 21, 39; Noren Trotman/NBA Photos, p. 35.

Cover Photo: AP/Wide World Photos

Interior Design: Richard Stalzer

CONTENTS

INTRODUCTION   4

CHARLES BARKLEY   6

DERRICK COLEMAN   10

DAVE DeBUSSCHERE   14

ELVIN HAYES   18

LARRY JOHNSON   22

KARL MALONE   26

KEVIN McHALE   30

DENNIS RODMAN   34

DOLPH SCHAYES   38

CHRIS WEBBER   42

CHAPTER NOTES   46

INDEX   48

INTRODUCTION

THE POWER FORWARD IS A relatively new position. Until the last few decades, power forwards in professional basketball did not exist.

Like all sports, pro basketball has changed in many ways. Metal rims with nets replaced peach baskets. A twenty-four-second shot clock was added to speed up the game. One of the biggest changes of all has been the rugged play of the big men in the paint. With opposing centers often neutralizing one another, a second big man has emerged to swat away shots and scrape rebounds off the glass. He is the power forward.

The power forward is a robust man. He is strong of mind and body. He must be able to hold his ground under the basket, to pound and be pounded by opponents. He must have the will to control his area of the court and grab the basketball when it comes his way. Playing power forward is dirty work. It is not a job for the soft player.

The NBA has become a game of bone-jarring slam dunks. It is the job of the power forward to administer those dunks, and to prevent his opponents from doing the same. He must be willing to sacrifice his body, to take a charge, to help out on a double-team, and to stop any opponent coming down the lane to score.

The power forward does not have to be a team leader, but he must play a team game. The power forward does not have to create great plays, but he must execute the play if it is created for him by a point guard.

The power forward does not have to be a big scorer, but he must be able to score when he has the open shot. He must be able to use his elbows and hips to get in position to receive an entry pass. Then, he must be able to turn and put the ball in the basket. A power forward must be a threat at both ends of the court.

Most of all, the power forward must grab rebounds and play defense. So much attention these days is given to scoring. What about the player who prevents the score? The player who blocks the shot? The player who pulls down the rebound? The public may not understand, but his teammates do, that he is just as valuable as any scorer.

The Boston Celtics of the mid-1980s, the Detroit Pistons of the late 1980s, and the New York Knicks of the early 1990s featured big front lines with strong power forwards. These teams showed that pro basketball can be won with defense. Other teams have since adopted similar strategies.

With so many great power forwards in the league today, and many more having just retired, it is nearly impossible to pick ten men and say they are the greatest power forwards in the history of the game. The ten we have selected certainly stand out, but there are at least a dozen more who would make someone's top ten list. Here is *our* list.

CAREER STATISTICS

Player	Years Played	Rebounds	Blocks*	FG%	FT%	PPG
CHARLES BARKLEY	1984–	10,311	818	.550	.738	23.3
DERRICK COLEMAN	1990–	3,762	686	.461	.771	19.6
DAVE DEBUSSCHERE	1962–1974	9,618	—	.432	.699	16.1
ELVIN HAYES	1968–1984	16,279	1,771	.452	.670	21.0
LARRY JOHNSON	1991–	3,479	163	.496	.771	19.6
KARL MALONE	1983–	9,733	756	.525	.722	26.0
KEVIN MCHALE	1980–1993	7,122	1,690	.554	.798	17.9
DENNIS RODMAN	1986–	9,441	481	.535	.589	8.0
DOLPH SCHAYES	1948–1964	11,256	—	.380	.843	18.2
CHRIS WEBBER	1993–	1,326	258	.527	.528	19.1

*Statistics for blocks were not kept by the NBA until the 1973–74 season.

CHARLES BARKLEY

THE SCORE WAS TIED. SIX minutes remained in the game. America West Arena in Phoenix, Arizona, was rocking. The Phoenix Suns and rival Los Angeles Lakers were engaged in another of their classic NBA Pacific Division battles.

During a time-out in the 1994 contest, Charles Barkley walked over to the scorer's table. A moment later, 1,500 miles away in a brick house on Moton Street, in Leeds, Alabama, the telephone rang.

"Hello, Granny! You watchin' the game?"

While the rest of the Suns discussed strategy in a huddle at the Phoenix bench, Barkley was on the phone with his grandmother, Johnnie Mickens. Then, after a moment, he was talking with his mother, Charcey Glenn. A buzzer sounded, signaling the end of the two-minute time-out. The Lakers and Suns returned to the court. "I love you, Mama," Charles said. "Gotta go now!"[1]

Barkley ran onto the court, then led his team down the stretch to a victory.

Charles Barkley is his own man. He is a team player, more interested in winning than in personal statistics, but he is also a unique individual, and he marches to his own drum. "Never been anyone like me," he says, "never will be."[2]

Charles Barkley was born February 20, 1963. He was raised by his mother and grandmother in a housing project in Leeds, and he was always told he could be whatever he wanted to be. When Charles was seven, he wanted to be Superman. He put on a homemade Superman cape and threw his pudgy body out of a second-story window. He

CHARLES BARKLEY

Using his great leaping ability, Charles Barkley rejects the shot of the opposing player. In his first year, Barkley was selected to the All-Rookie team.

suffered a concussion and soon after decided to take up basketball instead.

In the gym, he was teased by junior high teammates because he was shy, short, and overweight, and had a big head. Outside, he often stayed out until nearly midnight to get a chance to play on the court.

Barkley starred for Leeds High School because he hustled and wanted the ball more than anyone else. He won a scholarship to Auburn University, where he honed his skills, then was the fifth pick by the Philadelphia 76ers in the 1984 draft. He learned the pro game from superstars Julius Erving and Moses Malone, made the NBA All-Rookie team, and has been named to the All-NBA first or second team every year since.

During Barkley's first year with the Suns in 1993, he averaged 25.6 points and 12.2 rebounds a game and led them to the NBA Finals. He was rewarded with the NBA Most Valuable Player award. In 1996, Barkley was traded to the Houston Rockets.

At six-feet six-inches, 252 pounds, Barkley's nickname is Round Mound of Rebound. He bangs under the boards against taller opponents, but usually winds up with the ball because he wants it more.

"He's an unbelievable competitor," says former teammate Kevin Johnson, "and he does whatever it takes to win within reason—and sometimes even without a reason!"[3]

CHARLES BARKLEY

BORN: February 20, 1963, Leeds, Alabama.

HIGH SCHOOL: Leeds High School, Leeds, Alabama.

COLLEGE: Auburn University.

PRO: Philadelphia 76ers, 1984–1992; Phoenix Suns, 1992–1996; Houston Rockets, 1996– .

RECORDS: Most offensive rebounds in one quarter (11), one half (13).

Honors: NBA Most Valuable Player, 1993; All-NBA first team, 1988–1991, 1993.

Trying to shed the defender, Barkley looks for an easy layup. In 1993, Barkley won the NBA Most Valuable Player award.

DERRICK COLEMAN

THE TASK SEEMED OVERWHELMING. NEW Jersey Nets power forward Derrick Coleman was asked to hold his own against Philadelphia's massively built front line of Charles Barkley and Rick Mahorn.

Sure, Coleman was the top pick in the draft, and sure, he had played well his first thirteen games of the 1990 season, averaging 16.4 points and 10.2 rebounds a game. Derrick was still just a rookie, though. The 76ers surely would push him all around the Spectrum in Philadelphia, Pennsylvania.

It didn't happen that way. Coleman stood tall against the wily Barkley and brutish Mahorn, pounding the glass for the Nets. When the final buzzer sounded, and the Nets had won, Barkley and Mahorn walked off the court shaking their heads. Coleman had pulled down 23 rebounds and scored 28 points, leading the Nets to victory.

"From day one, I proved that I belong," Coleman said after the game. "I always had confidence in my ability. I know what I can do on the court."[1]

The rest of the league was finding out. When the season ended, Coleman had overcome a severely sprained ankle to win the NBA Rookie of the Year. Since then, he has developed into a tremendous talent, a punishing inside player with a soft shooting touch. The 76ers so admired Coleman's skills, that they acquired him in a trade in 1995.

Derrick Coleman was born June 21, 1967. He grew up in Mobile, Alabama, where he learned to shoot accurately by tossing a basketball between the limbs of two pecan trees in his grandmother's backyard. At the age of thirteen, he

Derrick Coleman heads downcourt, looking to make his next big play. In 1991, Coleman was named NBA Rookie of the Year.

moved to Detroit, Michigan, where he learned to dribble by turning off the basement lights in his uncle Robert and aunt Mary's home and bouncing the ball while walking back and forth between the wall and the furnace.

As a tall, skinny, left-hander, Coleman starred at Northern High School in Detroit, and the recruiting offers poured in. At Syracuse University, he established himself as one of the greatest college basketball players ever by becoming the first to accumulate 2,000 points, 1,500 rebounds, and 300 blocks in a career. He is the all-time NCAA leader with 1,537 rebounds.

The Nets found that Coleman did not lack for confidence when they drafted him No. 1 and he said, "I am the franchise. If you want somebody who is versatile and can play any position on the court, then I'm the man."[2]

At six-feet ten-inches, Coleman is a remarkable shooter and passer. He also runs the court well and makes his presence felt with thunderous slam dunks. Derrick hones his skills by showing up early for practice, then staying late shooting extra baskets and running laps.

"He's a great, great player," center Sam Bowie said in Coleman's first year. "He changes the game. I just hope the commissioner doesn't make him illegal."[3]

DERRICK COLEMAN

BORN: June 21, 1967, Mobile, Alabama.

HIGH SCHOOL: Northern High School, Detroit, Michigan.

COLLEGE: Syracuse University.

PRO: New Jersey Nets, 1990–1995; Philadelphia 76ers, 1995– .

HONORS: NBA Rookie of the Year, 1991.

Playing above the rim, Derrick Coleman looks to finish the shot. While playing at Syracuse University, Coleman pulled down more rebounds than any other player in college history.

DAVE DEBUSSCHERE

Dave DeBusschere was drafted by the Detroit Pistons in 1962. Two years later, he was named coach of the team.

DAVE DEBUSSCHERE

EVERYTHING WAS GOING WRONG FOR Dave DeBusschere. The New York Knicks and Boston Celtics were battling for the 1972 Eastern Conference title at Boston Garden, and DeBusschere was not helping the Knicks at all.

He spent most of the first quarter on the bench in foul trouble. He missed the entire second quarter because he took a salt tablet to prevent dehydration and the pill stuck in his throat. He had to dash to the dressing room, gagging and choking.

DeBusschere scored just 3 points in the first half. The underdog Knicks were losing. Something had to be done.

DeBusschere did it. He is not renowned for his offense, but he decided to shoot the ball in the third quarter. He scored 18 points. He made seven of eight shots, most of them long-range bombs, and the Celtics could not stop him. The Knicks won the game to advance to the NBA finals.

"When you're going like that, you want the ball, and the ball kept coming my way," DeBusschere told reporters after the game. "When you're going good, you have no idea how many points you have, although you know you have a lot."[1]

Dave DeBusschere averaged 16.1 points a game in his career, but his scoring was secondary to his dirty work—the rebounding, the picks and screens, the tenacious defending. He was a workhorse who banged under the basket with larger men, chomping on a stick of gum all the while.

Dave DeBusschere was born October 16, 1940. He was a gifted athlete as a boy growing up in Detroit, Michigan. He pitched a Little League team to a national championship. He led Austin Catholic High School to a city baseball title and state basketball title.

At the University of Detroit, DeBusschere pitched his baseball team to three straight NCAA playoff berths. On the court, he averaged nearly twenty-five points per game to lead the Titans to two NIT basketball berths and an NCAA tournament. He also pitched for the Chicago White Sox.

DeBusschere was selected in the 1962 draft by the Detroit Pistons, and he was so bright and shrewd that in his third year, at the age of twenty-four, he was named head coach of the team. He always made sure to name himself a starter for each game.

On December 19, 1968, DeBusschere was at home, hanging a framed picture of himself driving for a layup over New York Knicks center Walt Bellamy, when the telephone rang. DeBusschere was told that he had just been traded from the Pistons to the Knicks—for Walt Bellamy.

DeBusschere played an instrumental role in the Knicks' championship seasons of 1970 and 1973. In 1982, he was inducted into the Basketball Hall of Fame.

"Dave was always something to watch," said Knicks coach Red Holzman. "He was strong, a good shooter, a great rebounder, and he played defense."[2]

DAVE DEBUSSCHERE

BORN: October 16, 1940, Detroit, Michigan.
HIGH SCHOOL: Austin Catholic High School, Detroit, Michigan.
COLLEGE: University of Detroit.
PRO: Detroit Pistons, 1962–1968; New York Knicks, 1968–1974.
RECORDS: Youngest coach in NBA history.
HONORS: NBA All-Defensive first team, 1969–1974; Elected to
Naismith Memorial Basketball Hall of Fame, 1982.

DeBusschere was traded to the New York Knicks in 1968. In the
early 1970s, the Knicks' legendary lineup included Hall-of-Famer
Walt Frazier and captured two NBA championships.

ELVIN HAYES

ELVIN HAYES SCORED MORE THAN 27,000 points and grabbed more than 16,000 rebounds in a long sixteen-year career in the NBA. His greatest game, though, came in college.

The No. 1 ranked UCLA Bruins and the No. 2 ranked Houston Cougars met January 20, 1968, at the Houston Astrodome in the first college game played in a domed facility, in front of the largest crowd ever to witness a college basketball game, and with college basketball's first nationally televised audience watching.

The big matchup was at center, where Elvin Hayes took on giant seven-foot two-inch Lew Alcindor. The UCLA center would later change his name to Kareem Abdul-Jabbar. Alcindor, as he was known then, played well, scoring 15 points and grabbing 12 rebounds, but Hayes dominated inside, moving under, around, and over the Bruin center to score 39 points and pull down 15 rebounds. Houston won in an upset, 71-69.

Hayes was introduced to the nation that night, in what is still known as the Game of the Century. He capped his senior year by being named College Player of the Year. He was the first pick in the NBA draft, and his career took off like a rocket.

Elvin Hayes was born November 17, 1945. Growing up in tiny Rayville, Louisiana, Elvin never touched a basketball until eighth grade. It happened one day by a fluke. Elvin sat innocently in class when another student poked the girl in front of him. Thinking it was Elvin, she turned and stabbed him in the arm with her pencil. The teacher

ELVIN HAYES

In 1978, Hayes led the Bullets to their first-ever NBA championship. They defeated the Seattle Supersonics in seven games.

blamed Elvin and sent him to the gym. Elvin was small and unathletic, but he was put on the basketball team that day. He sat on the bench that year, the next, and the next, through his sophomore year of high school.

The summer before his junior year, Elvin practiced eight hours a day at the gym. On weekends, when the gym was closed, he shot by himself in his backyard, into a tin bucket he had nailed to a willow tree. He scored 1,200 points as a junior, 2,000 as a senior, and boosted Eula D. Britton High School to a state championship.

Hayes starred in college, and was nicknamed the Big E after the powerful aircraft carrier *Enterprise*. In his first season in the NBA, playing for the San Diego Rockets, Hayes led the league in shots attempted, shots made, points scored, and scoring average.

A year after the San Diego franchise moved to Houston, Hayes was traded to the Baltimore (later Washington) Bullets. He guided the Bullets to a 60-22 record and the 1975 NBA finals, but they were swept in four games by the Golden State Warriors. "An embarrassing and disastrous series," Hayes called it.[1] Vowing to return to the championship series, the Big E led his team to the 1978 finals. This time, the Bullets won the seventh game in Seattle to beat the SuperSonics for the title.

"People try to compare others to him," says Ted Nance, Houston's sports information director. "It's like trying to compare someone to Babe Ruth."[2]

ELVIN HAYES

BORN: November 17, 1945, Rayville, Louisiana.

HIGH SCHOOL: Eula D. Britton High School, Rayville, Louisiana.

COLLEGE: University of Houston.

PRO: San Diego Rockets, 1968–1971; Houston Rockets, 1971–1972; Baltimore Bullets, 1972–1973; Capital Bullets, 1973–1974; Washington Bullets, 1974–1981; Houston Rockets, 1981–1984.

RECORDS: NBA single-season record for most minutes played by a rookie (3,695) in 1968–1969.

HONORS: All-NBA first team, 1975, 1977, 1979. Elected to Naismith Memorial Basketball Hall of Fame (1989).

Hayes played in the NBA for sixteen years. He is third on the all-time list for field goals with 10,976, fourth for total points with 27,313, and fourth for rebounds with 16,279.

LARRY JOHNSON

Going up for the block, Larry Johnson attempts to stop Charles Barkley. Johnson was named Rookie of the Year in 1992.

IT WAS PAYBACK TIME. THE Detroit Pistons arrived at the Charlotte Coliseum in North Carolina in March 1992 to play the Hornets. Charlotte rookie Larry Johnson had a score to settle.

The day the Hornets made him the No. 1 selection in the NBA draft, Johnson was watching as Detroit's John Salley was being interviewed on television. "I heard Larry likes to talk," Salley said into the camera. "When he gets to the NBA, all that talk is going to stop."

Johnson took notice and wrote down Salley's name. "I remember stuff like that," he said.[1]

Johnson powered over Salley for 22 points, and held Salley to 9, and the Hornets upset the Pistons, 113-101. Payback complete.

Johnson dominated plenty of opponents on his way to claiming the NBA Rookie of the Year award. Since then, he has become a sheer force in the league.

Johnson is a rock-solid six-foot seven-inch, 250-pound bull, and his long arms span over seven feet. He talks trash with opponents, taunting them into mistakes. After a great play, he'll shadowbox downcourt, or he'll just stand under the basket, hands on hips, flashing his gold-toothed grin, amid the cheering. He had the tooth capped with gold by a dentist when he was eighteen. It cost him $200. "It's my trademark," Johnson says. "It's been big for me."[2]

Larry Johnson was born March 14, 1969, in Tyler, Texas. He grew up on Dixon Circle in south Dallas, where he broke into stores, played with guns, hung out with gang members, and went to bed hungry. Without a father, but with a loving mother who worked thirteen hours a day, six days a week, Larry knew about being poor. "If we could eat," he said, "we were happy."[3]

He learned to box in Golden Gloves tournaments, and those skills came in handy. In seventh grade, he was a big target at six-feet two-inches, 180 pounds. Knock him down on the basketball court, get respect. Enough kids tried. Larry was so strong he once ripped the hoop right off the backboard on a dunk. "That's still the talk of Dixon right there," says his best friend, Greg Williams. "Everybody just looked at that, and they knew then and there he was going to the league."[4]

Johnson played two years at Odessa Junior College, then transferred to the University of Nevada-Las Vegas, where he led the Rebels to a national championship his junior year and was named NCAA Player of the Year as a senior.

In 1994, Johnson signed a contract for $84 million over the next twelve seasons, an average of $7 million a year. He recently filmed twelve commercials for a shoe company in which he wears a flowery dress, wig, fake pearls and glasses, and plays a character called *Grandmama*. The commercials air regularly on television. "It was a lot of fun to shoot. Lot of fun, lot of fun," he says. "Grandmama is prime time."[5]

So is Larry Johnson. "I'm very impressed by Larry," San Antonio Spurs center David Robinson says. "He's a tremendous player."[6]

LARRY JOHNSON

BORN: March 14, 1969, Tyler, Texas.

HIGH SCHOOL: Skyline High School, Dallas, Texas.

COLLEGE: University of Nevada-Las Vegas.

PRO: Charlotte Hornets, 1991–1996; New York Knicks, 1996– .

HONORS: NBA Rookie of the Year, 1992.

Lining up his shot, Larry Johnson attempts to hit from outside. After a stellar career at the University of Nevada-Las Vegas, the Charlotte Hornets made Larry Johnson the first pick in the 1991 draft.

KARL MALONE

In order to get an open shot, Karl Malone puts the moves on Hakeem Olajuwon. The Utah Jazz have made the playoffs every year that Malone has been with the team.

KARL MALONE HAD BECOME A fan favorite. He was starting in his second straight All-Star Game, this one in 1989 at the Astrodome in Houston, Texas. His Utah Jazz teammate, John Stockton, would start alongside him at point guard for the Western All-Stars.

When Malone and Stockton team up, good things happen. The Texas crowd and a national television audience found this out as Stockton repeatedly passed inside to Malone for baskets. The Eastern All-Stars—Larry Bird, Charles Barkley, Patrick Ewing—could do nothing to stop it. Basket Malone, assist Stockton. Basket Malone, assist Stockton. It played over and over again like a broken record.

When the game ended, the West had won 143-134. Malone had racked up a game-high 28 points on 12-of-17 shooting, and pulled down 9 rebounds. Stockton had 17 assists, including a record 9 in the first quarter.

When Malone was presented the MVP award after the game, he held up the trophy, pointed at Stockton, and said, "I'll split this thing right down the middle with that little guy."[1] Malone enjoyed the All-Star Game so much that he's been back every year since.

Karl Malone was born July 24, 1963. He was one of eight children raised by their mother in a house in the woods of Summerfield, Louisiana. He learned to fish in nearby ponds, and hunt squirrels and deer with a shotgun. He spent too much time playing and not enough studying, and was ineligible to play basketball as a high school freshman. Karl joined the Summerfield High Rebels as a sophomore and led them to three consecutive state titles. College recruiting letters poured in even before Karl averaged 32.4 points and 18 rebounds a game his senior year. At Louisiana Tech, he developed a dominant inside game too powerful to stop.

Malone knew little about the Utah Jazz when they selected him with the thirteenth pick of the 1985 draft. He had never even been to the state of Utah. Karl had no trouble fitting in, though, as he came off the bench to get 8 points, 6 rebounds, and 4 steals in his first game as a pro.

At six-feet ten-inches, 260 pounds, Malone is a sturdy presence under the boards. By spending countless hours in the gym away from practice, he developed a superb touch on medium-range jumpers. His scoring average improved his first five years this way: 14.9, 21.7, 27.7, 29.1, and 31.0. It's no wonder that he has led the Jazz to the playoffs all ten years he's been with them. "Karl does most of the dirty work," says Stockton. "I just have to get him the ball."[2]

Malone still enjoys hunting and fishing, and has taken up another hobby—trucking. He owns an eighteen-wheel truck and wants to open a trucking company when he retires from basketball. In the meantime, like any great power forward, he likes pounding the ball down his opponent's throat. "The paint is where men are made. That's where I earn my living," he says. "Nobody ever takes me one-on-one. When one guy can stop me, that's when I retire."[3]

KARL MALONE

BORN: July 24, 1963, Summerfield, Louisiana.

HIGH SCHOOL: Summerfield High School, Summerfield, Louisiana.

COLLEGE: Louisiana Tech University.

PRO: Utah Jazz, 1985– .

HONORS: All-NBA first team, 1989–1995.

Battling in the paint, Malone is determined to get to the basket. Malone's talent and determination have made him a perennial All-Star.

KEVIN McHALE WAS MIDWAY THROUGH his third year with the Boston Celtics, in the middle of a game with the Milwaukee Bucks, when a thought struck him. He might, just might, break a personal record.

After the game on December 13, 1982, had ended, McHale was in the locker room when the statistics sheets arrived. He looked for his name, glanced at the "shots attempted" column, and saw the number—22. McHale had finally done it. In his 182nd game as a pro, he took at least twenty shots in a game. He finished a tidy 13-of-22 for 30 points.

Twenty shots a game is a benchmark for a "go-to" guy. The Celtics had Larry Bird. They didn't need McHale to shoot often. When he did, though, he usually made the shot.

McHale led the league in shooting percentage twice, and was in the top five several more times. Teamed with Bird, the Celtics had an unstoppable front court. McHale played thirteen years with the Celtics, and thirteen times the Celtics made the playoffs. It was no coincidence. McHale was a winner.

Kevin McHale was born December 19, 1957. He grew up among the trees and lakes of Hibbing, Minnesota, where hockey was the popular sport. Kevin was only the second best player on his Hibbing High School basketball team, but when the star broke his wrist early in Kevin's senior season, Kevin took control of the Blue Jackets, led them to the state championship game, and was selected Mr. Basketball in the state of Minnesota. He followed with four stellar years at

KEVIN MCHALE

Moving with the ball, Kevin McHale looks to make a big play. Because of McHale's hard work he was selected to NBA All-Defensive teams six times.

the University of Minnesota, where he led the Gophers in just about every statistical category.

Playing for the Celtics, McHale was known for his efficient scoring both inside and outside, and his left-handed shot blocking. He played such tenacious defense that he usually guarded the opposing team's best player, whether it was the shooting guard or center.

The capacity crowds at Boston Garden considered Bird a living legend, while McHale was merely a sidekick. McHale scored 56 points on March 3, 1985, to set a Celtics record. Nine days later, Bird broke the record by scoring 60. "Kevin's attitude was, 'So what?'" said Celtics center Robert Parish. "It was typical, really, of Kevin's whole career. He was always going to be overshadowed by God."[1]

McHale cared more about winning, anyway. He was named to the NBA All-Defensive first or second team six times. He won the NBA Sixth Man award in 1984 and 1985, and after that, he was just too talented to keep on the bench at the start of the game. When he rose up to take a shot, his arms seemed to stretch forever.

"Without a doubt, he was the most difficult low-post player to defend once he made the catch in the history of the league," says TV commentator and former coach Hubie Brown. "He was totally unstoppable because of his quickness, diversification of moves, and long arms that gave him an angle to release the ball."[2]

KEVIN McHALE

BORN: December 19, 1957, Hibbing, Minnesota.

HIGH SCHOOL: Hibbing High School, Hibbing, Minnesota.

COLLEGE: University of Minnesota.

PRO: Boston Celtics, 1980–1993.

HONORS: NBA Sixth Man Award, 1984, 1985; All-NBA first team,
1987.

Throughout his career, the Celtics could count on Kevin McHale to
make his shots. McHale led the NBA in shooting percentage twice.

DENNIS RODMAN

HIS NAVEL IS PIERCED. TATTOOS cover his body. His hair color has been purple, red, blond, and blue. His nickname is The Worm.

Dennis Rodman is the most outrageous player the NBA has ever had. Probably the best rebounder ever, too. In a game at the Alamodome in San Antonio, Texas, on January 22, 1994, Rodman displayed his great ability in a big way. He slipped around the Dallas Mavericks' Sean Rooks to grab a rebound. He cut under Tim Legler to get another. He jumped over Jamal Mashburn, and out-fought Jimmy Jackson for two more. He sneaked and slithered and "wormed" his way to 32 rebounds that night—the most any player made in a single game that season.

Rodman is just six-feet eight-inches, and a wiry 210 pounds—small for a rebounder—but nobody pounds the boards like him, and few match him defensively. Since joining the Detroit Pistons as the twenty-seventh pick in the 1986 draft out of tiny Southeastern Oklahoma State University, Rodman has specialized in the blue-collar work of the game. He is strong and quick, with maybe the best hands and reflexes in the league.

In 1995, with the Spurs, Rodman won his fourth consecutive rebounding title. With the Chicago Bulls in 1996, he won his fifth. He wins them by a wide margin, too, usually by more than four rebounds per game. In 1995, for example, he averaged 16.8 boards per game. Denver Nuggets center Dikembe Mutombo was second at 12.5, Orlando Magic center Shaquille O'Neal third at 11.4, and New York Knicks center Patrick Ewing fourth at 11.0.

DENNIS RODMAN

Dennis Rodman is the best rebounder in basketball. In 1996, he won his fifth consecutive rebounding title.

"I'm so feisty," Rodman says. "I'm a lion, a tiger, an octopus, a shark. I attack anything."[1]

Dennis Rodman was born May 13, 1961. He grew up in Dallas, and lived with another family during high school. He never played high school basketball. He decided to try the game in college, just for fun. He discovered he liked it, at least the rebounding, anyway.

Rodman spent seven years with the Pistons, leading them to two NBA titles. In 1996, he was able to do the same with Michael Jordan and the Bulls. And he does it with a flair never before seen.

"He's almost like a cartoon character, a super hero," says former Washington Bullets forward Kenny Walker.

"No doubt he has a loose screw," says Sacramento Kings guard Mitch Richmond.

"He thinks the ball belongs to him," says Bullets general manager Wes Unseld.

"He spends the whole 24 seconds trying to figure out how he can get the rebound—at both ends," says Boston Celtics guard Dee Brown.[2]

Some people appreciate Dennis Rodman, some do not, but everyone, it seems, has an opinion. And Dennis, it seems, doesn't care—as long as he gets the rebound.

DENNIS RODMAN

BORN: May 13, 1961, Trenton, New Jersey.

HIGH SCHOOL: South Oak Cliff High School, Dallas, Texas.

COLLEGE: Southeastern Oklahoma State University.

PRO: Detroit Pistons, 1986–1993; San Antonio Spurs, 1993–1995; Chicago Bulls, 1995– .

HONORS: NBA Defensive Player of the Year, 1990, 1991.

Rodman wards off opposing players to get the loose ball. His fine defensive play has made him a big part of three world championship teams.

DOLPH SCHAYES

DOLPH SCHAYES WAS FRUSTRATED. HIS Syracuse Nationals were losing the deciding seventh game of the 1955 NBA finals on their home court. Losing badly, too. It was halftime, and the Nats trailed Fort Wayne by sixteen points.

The home court advantage had been big in the series. Each team had won its three games at home. Whatever the reason for his team's struggle in Game 7, Schayes was thankful of one thing—the shot clock. Syracuse owner Danny Biasone convinced the league before the season to institute a twenty-four-second clock.

A year earlier, Fort Wayne could have stalled and run out the clock. In this game, Fort Wayne had to shoot. Schayes and his teammates played solid defense in the second half and made a late charge to win the title, 92-91.

"If the old time situation still prevailed," Schayes recalls, "we wouldn't have had a chance to come back to win that game."[1]

Schayes played sixteen years of pro basketball, fourteen with the NBA's Nationals. He led the Nats to the playoffs every year. Only once in his first dozen seasons did Schayes fail to finish among the top 7 NBA players in both scoring and rebounding. He was an easy choice for induction into the Basketball Hall of Fame in 1972.

Adolph Schayes was born May 19, 1928. He grew up in New York City, where he spent much of his time on the basketball playgrounds. A whiz in school, he enrolled at New York University at the age of sixteen, and made his playing debut two months later at Madison Square Garden in a game against rival Notre Dame.

DOLPH SCHAYES

Dolph Schayes was a star of the National Basketball League. He was signed by the Syracuse Nationals in 1948. He played his final season with the team when they moved to Philadelphia and became the 76ers in 1963.

By his senior year in college, Schayes stood six feet eight inches and had developed a deadly two-handed set shot that couldn't be stopped. In 1948, he was a first-round draft pick by both the hometown New York Knicks of the Basketball Association of America, and the Nationals, who were in the rival National Basketball League. The Knicks offered a contract for $5,000. The Nats offered $7,500. Dolph packed his car and drove to upstate New York to join the Nats. By the following season, the NBL and BAA merged to form the National Basketball Association, and Schayes played against the best athletes of his era.

Schayes appeared in eleven NBA All-Star Games, including the first one in 1951 at the Boston Garden, where he was the leading rebounder, with 14, as the East beat the West.

Danny Schayes, Dolph's son, has played center for the Phoenix Suns and other teams for several years in the NBA. "He's the ultimate team player," Dolph says of his son. "He makes everybody on his team play better when he's on the court."[2]

Dolph could easily have been talking about himself.

DOLPH SCHAYES

BORN: May 19, 1928, New York City, New York.

HIGH SCHOOL: DeWitt Clinton High School, Bronx, New York.

COLLEGE: New York University.

PRO: Syracuse Nationals, 1948–1963; Philadelphia 76ers, 1963–1964.

HONORS: All-NBA first team, 1952–1955, 1957–1958. Elected to Naismith Memorial Basketball Hall of Fame, 1972.

Schayes drives against the Knicks' Ernie Vandeweghe in this 1952 Eastern Division playoff game. Schayes' Syracuse Nationals would lose the best-of-five series. This game was played at a New York City armory.

CHRIS WEBBER

Knifing through the defense, Chris Webber avoids his opponents and tries to lay the ball in. Webber won the Rookie of the Year award in 1994.

CHRIS WEBBER

THE FAB FIVE TRAILED BY two. There was a mad scramble for the ball. Eleven seconds remained when Chris Webber grabbed it in front of his team's bench. He turned toward the official and called a time-out.

It was the most horrifying moment of Chris Webber's basketball life.

Webber was among five high school stars who joined the University of Michigan a year earlier and led the Wolverines to the NCAA championship game. They were dubbed the Fab Five, and they were back in the title game for the second time, this time to win it. Webber had scored 23 points and grabbed 11 rebounds against mighty North Carolina, and now he had the ball. The problem was, Michigan had no time-outs left. Webber forgot that.

Michigan was assessed a technical foul for calling a time-out. North Carolina was awarded two free throws and possession. The Tar Heels won the title, 77-71. Chris Webber left school the next day. It was time for him to join the NBA. "I had to reach my dream," he said, "because it was burning inside me."[1]

Chris draws attention wherever he goes. It's been that way since he was in the eighth grade, and a television crew followed him around school all day, then that afternoon to the gym, where he scored 64 points in a game, with fifteen of his baskets coming on dunks.

Chris Webber was born March 1, 1973. He grew up in Detroit, Michigan, where he played basketball for hours every day. As a senior at Detroit Country Day High School in Birmingham, Michigan, Chris was named Mr. Basketball for the state of Michigan after leading his team to the second of two straight state championships.

Webber dominated in college. Now he dominates in the pros. "I'll say this," Webber boasts, "I don't care who I'm playing against. I'm betting on myself."[2]

The first pick in the 1993 draft by the Golden State Warriors, Webber was the youngest player in the league when he averaged 17.5 points, 9.1 rebounds, 2.2 blocks, and was named NBA Rookie of the Year.

After a bitter feud with former Warriors coach Don Nelson, Webber was traded in 1994 to the Washington Bullets, where he was reunited with Juwan Howard, another of Michigan's Fab Five. Webber fully expects to lead the Bullets to the NBA title.

"Chris is a terrific talent," said Bullets coach Jim Lynam. "He's a young guy with an explosiveness to his game."[3]

At six-feet ten-inches, 250 pounds, Webber can do it all. He fights centers for rebounds, makes smart passes, runs the court well, and has good range with a soft touch. His tenacious attitude should make him a force in the twenty-first century.

Even Don Nelson, who had trouble coaching Webber, sees big things in Webber's future. "I truly believe," says Nelson, "that Chris can be the best power forward ever."[4]

Chris Webber

Born: March 1, 1973, Detroit, Michigan.

High School: Detroit Country Day High School, Birmingham, Michigan.

College: University of Michigan.

Pro: Golden State Warriors, 1993–1994; Washington Bullets, 1994– .

Honors: NBA Rookie of the Year, 1994.

Chris Webber is known for his thundering dunks. He once scored 64 points in a high school basketball game with 15 of his baskets coming on slams.

CHAPTER NOTES

Charles Barkley

1. Chris Cobbs, "Sir Charles' Real Coaches," *Phoenix Gazette*, May 30, 1994, p. 1.
2. Mark Jacobson, "Chuck," *Esquire*, May 1993, p. 93.
3. Clare Martin, "Sir Charles In Charge," *Hoop Magazine*, January 1993, p. 6.

Derrick Coleman

1. Jan Hubbard, "The Franchise," *Newsday*, December 22, 1990, p. 11.
2. Jack Curry, "Coleman: Rich, Gifted and Loving It," *The New York Times*, December 10, 1990, p. C1.
3. Hubbard, p. 11.

Dave DeBusschere

1. Phil Pope, "A Hero? The Man in the Trench," *New York Daily News*, April 25, 1972, p. 69.
2. Sam Goldaper, "DeBusschere—Basketball Hero of Two Cities," *The New York Times*, February 1, 1974, p. L22.

Elvin Hayes

1. David DuPree, "After 16 Years, It's Still E—as in End," *Washington Post*, April 4, 1984, p. 4.
2. Doug Mitchell, "He Made It Look Easy," *Houston Post*, December 19, 1993, p. 1.

Larry Johnson

1. Chris Tomasson, "Johnson Puts Power in Hornets' Sting," *Hoop Magazine*, January 1993, p. 6.
2. David Tarrant, "Courting Success from South Dallas to the NBA," *Dallas Morning News*, February 6, 1994, p. 2.
3. Ron Green, Jr., "Basketball Pulled Star Up, Away," *Charlotte Observer*, October 1, 1994, p. 8.
4. Ibid.
5. Tarrant, p. 2.
6. Tomasson, p. 10.

Karl Malone

1. Jeff Savage, *Sports Great Karl Malone* (Springfield, N.J.: Enslow Publishers, 1995), p. 51.

2. Fran Blinebury, "Malone-Stockton Partnership Has Done Everything Except Win a Title," *Houston Chronicle*, May 27, 1994, p. 2.

3. Savage, p. 61.

Kevin McHale

1. Jackie MacMullan, "Low-Key in Low Post," *Boston Globe*, January 30, 1994, p. 87.

2. Bob Ryan, "The Moves Were One of a Kind," *Boston Globe*, May 27, 1993, p. 73.

Dennis Rodman

1. David DuPree, "What's It All About, Dennis," *USA Today*, February 2, 1994, p. C1.

2. Ibid p. C1.

Dolph Schayes

1. Dan Herbst, "Hoop Legends—Dolph Schayes," *Hoop Magazine*, April 1991, p. 72.

2. Ibid, p. 70.

Chris Webber

1. Jerry Bembry, "Webber Is Still a Warrior," *Arizona Sun*, November 25, 1994, p. 8.

2. Ibid.

3. Karen Goldberg, "Webber's Brash Style of Play Breeds Success at Every Level," *Washington Times*, November 18, 1994, p. 1.

4. Norm Frauenheim, "Warriors' Webber Voted Rookie of the Year," *Arizona Republic*, May 4, 1994, p. 1.

INDEX

A

Abdul-Jabbar, Kareem (Lew
    Alcindor), 18

B

Barkley, Charles, 6–9, 10, 27
Bellamy, Walt, 16
Biasone, Danny, 38
Bird, Larry, 27, 30, 32
Bowie, Sam, 12
Brown, Dee, 36
Brown, Hubie, 32

C

Coleman, Derrick, 10–13

D

DeBusschere, Dave, 14–17

E

Enterprise, 20
Erving, Julius, 8
Ewing, Patrick, 27, 34

H

Hayes, Elvin, 18–21
Holzman, Red, 16
Howard, Juwan, 44

J

Jackson, Jimmy, 34
Johnson, Kevin, 8
Johnson, Larry, 22–25

L

Legler, Tim, 34
Lynam, Jim, 44

M

Mahorn, Rick, 10
Malone, Karl, 26–29
Malone, Moses, 8
Mashburn, Jamal, 34
McHale, Kevin, 30–33
Mutombo, Dikembe, 34

N

Nance, Ted, 20
Nelson, Don, 44

O

O'Neal, Shaquille, 34

P

Parish, Robert, 32

R

Richmond, Mitch, 36
Robinson, David, 24
Rodman, Dennis, 34–37
Rooks, Sean, 34

S

Salley, John, 23
Schayes, Danny, 40
Schayes, Dolph, 38–41
Stockton, John, 27

U

Unseld, Wes, 36

W

Walker, Kenny, 36
Webber, Chris, 42–45